Love

Fruit of the Spirit

LOVE

YOUR DAILY MEDITATION

SISTER IRINI

Bible references: New Revised Standard Version Updated Edition (NRSVUE) from bible gateway.com

Cover Design: Deposit Photos
Editing: SEASEM Publications

SEASEM PUBLICATIONS
publications@seasem.org

As the Father has loved me, so I have loved you;
abide in my love.

John 15:9

Contents

Introduction

Each one of us is called to love, joy, peace, patience, kindness, generosity, faithfulness, gentleness, and self-control (Galatians 5:22-23). These are the fruit of the Spirit; positive outcomes of living true to the Spirit of God inside us. But what are they and how can we actively live out the fruit of the Spirit in our daily lives?

Beyond Everyday Virtues

At the heart of this series of meditation books is the understanding that the fruit of the Spirit are not simply ethical behaviours or moral goals. They are the manifestations of the Holy Spirit's work within us that transforms us into the likeness of Jesus Christ. Unlike virtues we might strive for through our own efforts, these fruit are a grace, a gift from God that deepens our relationship with God. They are divine energies that assist us to 'become participants of the divine nature.' (2 Peter 1:4)

Divine Energies

Divine energies are the way God reveals God's self in the world. Unlike the essence of God, which is beyond our comprehension, divine energies allow us to experience God's presence and action in our lives. These energies are uncreated, timeless and eternal, flowing from God's being, within us and about us, drawing us closer to God and to our true selves.

Living the Fruit

The fruit of the Spirit are direct outcomes of our proximity to God inside us. The more available to the Spirit we become, the more the divine energies of the Holy Spirit transform us. This book offers you thirty days of bathing in those energies. Through daily meditations on scripture, prayer and practical exercise, you spend time with God, creating rich soil that enable the Holy Spirit to transform your life. The personal revelation you receive will enhance how you relate to God, with others and yourself. By opening to the Spirit of God this way, your life will positively change as your soul's light increasingly reflects the divinity inside you.

Fruitful Change

Read how these meditations on the Word of God have been blessing people.

Betty's Renewal Betty found the meditations simple yet profoundly beautiful. The experience inspired her to travel to America from Australia for Easter to join her favourite preacher's ministry. The fruit of faithfulness, empowered by God's love and Word provided for Betty's dreams. And the fruit of Love has helped her branch out into Christian community and fellowship in a new way.

Tracy's Open Heart Tracy and her husband faced repeated tension in their marriage. The meditations helped 're-centre' Tracy to open her heart to her husband. He responded favourably, and almost instantly their relationship was transformed. The peace of Christ strengthened their love and entered their ongoing communication.

Angela's Patience Through the daily mediations, Angela realised that patience was absent in her upbringing, affecting her relationships. This revelation, fuelled by the power of the Holy Spirit, birthed the fruit of patience in Angela. Out of this revelation, faith and courage grew in her, and family relations were mended and deepened.

Anita's Conviction: Coming from a New Age background, Anita found herself embracing the meditations but feeling resistant and fearful when invited to defend the gospel. A church reading on the Apostle Thomas confirmed her personal revelation through the Word that day. She saw the works of the Holy Spirit then reinforcing her faith journey and the joy of God entered her, overcoming any fear and doubt.

Kathleen's Direction: New to Jesus, Kathleen realised through the daily scripture and prayer that her calling lay beyond her chosen field of psychotherapy. Part way through the meditations she retired, declaring 'It wasn't right and I just needed to let it go.' Kathleen knew she was called to serve in a different way. As she embraced the Holy Spirit's work in her, her life was redirected towards a deepening of her relationship with God. Her faith was strengthened and she met the change with courage and conviction.

Siyu's Healing After a painful relationship ending, Siyu found solace in the daily meditations, experiencing the Word of God and God's love afresh: 'I'm trusting the healing process and trusting God.' By letting the Spirit lead her, Siyu encountered surprising conversations with strangers that gave her comfort and led her into new spiritual fellowship. Her Christian faith was lit as she declared trust in God who heals and restores.

These testimonies declare power of living and walking in the Spirit as we remain faithful to the true vine that is Jesus Christ. More than intellectual exercises; the daily mediations open us to the divine grace God wants to bestow upon our life.

What to Expect

When you embark upon these meditations, you can expect change. Expect spiritual and emotional growth, and a richer, deeper relationship with God inside you. Notice your increased empathy, compassion and forgiveness. Be aware of how your personal relationships are blessed, and how the way you connect with people in general changes.

Your speech will be more considered. There will be increased stillness and silence with a desire towards sincerity.

This beauty that is authenticity stems from the grace God bestows upon us as we turn more and more towards the uncreate light within us. You will notice this growing sense of authenticity as God invites you to be increasingly and unapologetically, simply yourself in the divine energies.

With this simplicity of truth comes a heightened sense of inner peace, a renewed motivation towards acts of kindness and service, and a shift in the way you view the world towards love and positivity. Nuances of change specific to your own life and personality will emerge. God's divine love will draw out of you the best of you, and free you from limitations you have in love. Be prepared to say yes to these changes. They may be unfamiliar at first but the rewards are sublime.

Divine Reading

Here's how to approach your meditation. Divine reading, known as *Lectio Divina*, invites you into a deeply contemplative engagement with scripture. This fourfold path will be the jewel of your meditation experience with God.

1. **Read** Approach the daily scripture as you would a dear friend—with an open heart. Slowly read the passage, reverently whispering it aloud multiple times.

2. **Meditate** Now, gently reflect on the passage. This is an almost peripheral state of consciousness rather than a piercing analysis. The passage floats in awareness inviting you to notice how it interacts with aspects of your life. Observe any feelings or emotions that arise here, letting

them rise and fall without following in thought too far.

3. **Pray** Pray the prayer provided or respond to the passage with your own prayer. Then ask God, 'What do you have for me?' Here, you are opening to personal revelation that is unique to you. Pray and listen for a response. Notice any imagery that appears or spontaneous realisations. You will know the Word of God by its interruption in your process, by the newness it brings, the growth it inspires, the 'flavour' of the thought being different to your everyday thinking and the command of it. Remember, God never criticises, bullies, or hurts. God will only ever illuminate, reveal, guide or lead you for your good.

4. **Contemplate** With your heart longing to be met, the Spirit of God will respond. Rest now in the presence of God, allowing any revelation to find home in your heart.

In sublime contemplation, the mind slips away, the body ceases to protect, the world quietens as you become a spiritual being. Tears may release the joy of your union with God. Commit to the invitation God gives you. You might give thanks now, ask Jesus for forgiveness, open to healing, praise God or simply rest in the divine presence.

Practice

This is where the fruit of the Spirit is lived and shared. Practical exercises are given, allowing God the great adventure of participating in you taking the divine illumination into the world. As part of your daily practice you may like to keep a journal. This is particularly helpful for remembering God's word to you and recording any insights into the application of the Word in your life.

Obstacles

Do not be alarmed if you encounter obstacles to your meditations. And remember that the daily rhythm is a guide only. Go at God's pace, which might not be daily. Here are some examples of potential obstacles:

1. **Mistaking Divine Reading for Bible Study** Being caught up in what words mean or scriptural context, keeps you in the head rather than the heart. Let go of study and biblical analysis for the heart to open to divine leading.

2. **Ignoring Life Context** Remember your life context. Be mindful of how the Bible passage relates to certain aspects of your life, and notice the feelings, thoughts and emotions that arise at this time.

3. **Being Cut Off from Emotions** It is important to acknowledge emotions, even the uncomfortable or painful ones. Without dwelling on them, notice how they add to your life context in relation to the scripture passage.

4. **Hurrying** Slow down. Divine reading is not a race but a contemplation. Trust in God's timing. Revelation may not happen in the meditation but days or even weeks later.

5. **Be Kind** How you know and experience God is unique to you. Be kind with yourself in the daily process. Give yourself every measure of harmonious support, even if you fall asleep! Sometimes God simply wants you to rest in the Spirit.

6. **Doubting and Skepticism** Of all the obstacles to God's grace, doubt and skepticism are the most damaging. 'Did I really hear that word?' 'Am I making it up?' 'Was it real?'

Scepticism immediately separates us from God in the moment. Any word God has for us is lost to doubt. Please, allow God, and if you have doubts, take them to a spiritual director or companion, pray on them again or check scripture for a precedent.

7. **Limiting God** It may be tempting to stop the meditations after one revelation. You received a word from God, and amazed by the insight in your life, you rest content in the meditative success. The Holy Spirit continues to do works in and for us. And we must say, 'Yes, here am I God.' The fruit of the Spirit is adventuring to make of your soul a permanent home for divine illumination and for the fruit of the Spirit. Let your prayer be, 'More, Holy Spirit, give me more!'

Love

In the way of all fruit of the Spirit, divine love is both the instrument of our spiritual journey towards our Christ-like nature, and the end result of our divinisation—our divine character. Divine love caresses the soul into becoming one with itself, transforming the soul by God's touch.

As you enter into meditation with divine love, you will notice its power to make right all that is wrong, to open all that is closed, to bless all that unsettles, and to heal spiritual pain, and often emotional and physical pain. As you embrace God's love, you become God's love, able to see this love in every person and to be this love for every person. This month of daily meditations will grace you with such sweetness towards the highest blessing of love; yours to claim and to become.

The Invitation

As you meet these meditations, you are invited to trust that the Spirit of God inside you has led you here, anticipating your readiness to receive divine impartation. Expect to meet divine energies. And whether these are your first steps towards understanding the Spirit's work in your life or you are here to cultivate a richer faith, let your heart be open and rejoice in the raiment of God's transformative authority as the ineffable Holy One meets the blush of your soul in Love.

May the light of all glories bless you and keep you. And may you, having put on the light of Christ, become its very illumination in the world.

Sister Irini

Love

Your Daily Meditation

Day 1

Fruit of the Spirit

The fruit of the Spirit is love, joy, peace, patience,
kindness, generosity, faithfulness, gentleness,
and self-control.

Galatians 5:22-23

Prayer

Come Holy Spirit, Come. Fill me with the seeds of your good fruit that I may labour in your might and your mind and your Spirit for all eternity. Fill me with your glory that I may glorify you and bend to you my will now and forever. O Holy Spirit, let the seeds of your fruit in me feed the hungry and quench the thirst of those in need of living waters. Amen.

Daily Love Practice

What do you have for me?

Give yourself space today to reflect on love.
Notice what God brings to you for attention.
Pray specifically into that area of your life, of love that needs God's blessing.

Day 2

Love the Lord Your God

You shall love the Lord your God with all your heart and with all your soul and with all your might.

Deuteronomy 6:5

Prayer

Lord, see my heart now. Look into me and know my love sincere. Hear now the cry of my soul that wants you only, for you are my God and I love you Lord. Amen.

Daily Love Practice

Spend time today reflecting on how you love God.
Take time to write down all the ways. Notice what the Spirit of God inside you brings to your attention after reading the scripture a few times, and praying.
Be open to loving God in a new way.

Day 3

Love Your Neighbour

You shall love your neighbour as yourself.

Matthew 22:39

Prayer

Lord, let me love my neighbour in difficult times and in easy. Let me love them in their wealth and in their poverty, in their silence and their noise, in their ways that are familiar and different. O God, let me love my neighbour as your Son, our Saviour Jesus Christ. Amen.

Daily Love Practice

Today, love on your neighbour in a new way.
Offer them the hospitality, the attention, the prayer, anything that God shows you they need to feel the love of Christ in their life.

Day 4

Keep the Commandments

If you love me, you will keep my commandments.

John 14:15

Prayer

Jesus, raise me up in your commandments. Help me in my weakness, to stand righteous in you. In all ways, let me have ears to hear and a heart open to your Word. Amen.

Daily Love Practice

Familiarise yourself with Christ's commandments.*
Reflect on those the Spirit identifies as needing attention.
What are the commandments that need more love from you?
Pray for the Spirit of God inside you to bring change in that area, and notice the change in your life.

*See Appendix A

Day 5

Defend the Gospel

Those who proclaim Christ from goodwill do so out of love, knowing that I have been put here for the defence of the gospel.

Philippians 1:16

Prayer

Jesus, let your words be upon my tongue that I may speak, defend, know and glorify you. Praising you, rejoicing you, uplifting your Holy name before others, let me share in your wisdom and your breath as I speak and defend the living gospel. Amen.

Daily Love Practice

Defending the gospel is one of the great tests of faith. Today, as you reflect upon this scripture consider how you speak about your faith and the gospel of Jesus Christ. Read the verse aloud and prepare for the Holy Spirit to bring you an opportunity to defend the good news of the gospel.

Day 6

Abide in Light

Whoever loves a brother or sister abides in the light,
and in such a person there is no cause for stumbling.

1 John 2:10

Prayer

Lord, on this day, let me open my heart to those you bring before me. Let me see them through your eyes. And in seeing them, let me love them. Let me extend this love into my family, God, through your strength and through your wisdom, through your mercy and compassion, make straight my paths, always in your light. Amen.

Daily Love Practice

Today, let the Spirit of God bring to mind someone in need of your love. Whether friend or stranger, find a way today to reach out to them with a loving word or gesture; one that comes from the heart and from your union with God.

Day 7

Have A Humble Mind

Finally, all of you, have unity of spirit, sympathy, love for one another, a tender heart, and a humble mind.

1 Peter 3:8

Prayer

Come Holy Spirit, make of me humility. In the tenderness of my heart, in the loving of another, in the deeds you set me to, in the comings and goings of my life, in every thought and every word, let me be bent before you Lord that you can make of me what you will. Amen.

Daily Love Practice

Today, is a day of gratitude. What intimacy of faith does God inspire in your faith? What has God delivered you from? What promise has God fulfilled? What has Jesus healed? How have the Holy Spirit gifts enriched another? Today give thanks, ending with, 'Make of me a humble mind.'

Day 8

Love in Deed and Truth

Little children, let us love not in word or speech but in deed and truth.

1 John 3:18

Prayer

Happy is my heart Lord, knowing that you have filled me with your loving truth. Let me honour you in ways that set a guard over falsities, ever bringing forth from me a melody attuned to heavenly trumpets that herald,
'Here is one who loves in deed, and in truth.' Amen.

Daily Love Practice

Today, your heart lives anew in God's truth. Keep watch on your tongue, on your intentions, on your behaviours and on your thoughts. Notice deceit. Catch a lie before it is spoken.Act from honest love and celebrate your authenticity in Christ in the world.

Day 9

Free From Money

Keep your lives free from the love of money, and be content with what you have, for he himself has said, 'I will never leave you or forsake you.'

Hebrew 13:5

Prayer

Every day, in every way God, you are my provision. You are my need, my love, my satisfaction. You Lord are my everything. In you I am fulfilled. Amen.

Daily Love Practice

Memorise the above prayer. Notice how often your thoughts turn to money today or financial gain, security, concerns or hopes. Stop, and be with God. Speak this prayer aloud as you feel and pray its truth.

Day 10

Love One Another

This is my commandment, that you love one another as I have loved you.

John 15:12

Prayer

Lord, examine me for your love. Find within me seeds of your living truth. Let me not be found wanting. In finding your love in me, I pray it makes of me one who loves as you have loved. This I pray in your holy name, Jesus Christ, Amen.

Daily Love Practice

It is easy to love those we like, those who like us, and those who are like us. Today, look a little farther afield. Bring that glorious love of Christ to the one who is not like you, who is not a friend, the stranger, the wrong doer, the lost soul. Whether by prayer, by greeting, by silent acknowledgement in the heart, today give them the gift of Christ's love in you.

Day 11

Genuine Love

Let love be genuine; hate what is evil;
hold fast to what is good.

Romans 12:9

Prayer

O Lord, thank you for your love that casts out all evil. Thank you for redeeming my past, for helping me know what is good and how to hold fast to that good. Thank you for your Holy Spirit, and for your Son, Jesus who saves me. Amen.

Daily Love Practice

Think of a time when you were caught in the snares of wrongdoing, whether through your own behaviours or by the acts of another or others. Now cast God's loving light upon that time. Read the scripture gently out loud and repeat the prayer softly until it brings you forward to the present day. Notice how all things are redeemed through Christ.

Day 12

Without Love There Is Nothing

If I speak in the tongues of humans and of angels but do not have love, I am a noisy gong or a clanging cymbal. And if I have prophetic powers and understand all mysteries and all knowledge and if I have all faith so as to remove mountains but do not have love, I am nothing.

1 Corinthians 13:1-2

Prayer

Search me God for you know me. Search me for love. And where you find it absent, fill me. Fill me with your love. Let the fullness of your love permeate my being. And let all gifts of your grace, and all the ways you let me serve you in the world be an outpouring of your love. Amen.

Daily Love Practice

What are you proud of in yourself? Let God's love fill that thing? Bathe in that love. If it is absent, pray for God to fill that space with divine love so that pride is replaced with deep gratitude that you have God's favour in that area. Notice how that aspect of yourself is given now to serve God.

Day 13

Love the Saints

I have heard of your faith in the Lord Jesus and your love toward all the saints.

Ephesians 1:15

Prayer

Yes, Lord. Let me love all believers set apart for your purposes. Let my faith lend itself in prayer to testify and uphold those ones whose lives are dedicated to you God. Amen.

Daily Love Practice

There are canonised saints in the Church, and when Paul is writing, his use of the term 'saints' refers to all believers in Christ. Think of a saint you know or have heard of and consider yourself a fellow believer with that saint. In what ways are you alike? What might the saint offer you? Pray love for all believers in Christ, saints and Saints of the Church.

Day 14

Commune With The Holy Spirit

The grace of the Lord Jesus Christ, the love of God, and the communion of the Holy Spirit be with all of you.

2 Corinthians 13:13

Prayer

May my breath breathe the Holy Spirit. May my conviction bring the Holy Spirit to bear upon any situation that needs the fine point of God's power. Amen.

Daily Love Practice

When the Holy Spirit comes upon you, the miraculous power of the heavens opens to you. 'Come Holy Spirit. Come!' Let you and the Spirit be one. Ignite your life today with a faith filled move of the Spirit. Task yourself something new, something fearful, something grand that only by communion with the Holy Spirit may you step forward in victory.

Day 15

Love Christ

Who will separate us from the love of Christ?
Will affliction or distress or persecution or famine or nakedness or peril or sword?

Romans 8:35

Prayer

Not my enemies Lord, nor my friends; not my family, nor my loved ones will ever separate me from you Jesus.
You are my yesterday, today and tomorrow. Amen

Daily Love Practice

Many in the Christian world wear the crown of martyrdom, having died for their faith. We may not meet these extreme circumstances but there are everyday relationships, encounters and activities that may try to separate us from Christ. Consider what might do this in your life and how you respond in Christ's defence, and stand for your faith.

Day 16

Without Seeing

Although you have not seen him, you love him;
and even though you do not see him now,
you believe in him and and rejoice with an indescribable
and glorious joy.

1 Peter 1:8

Prayer

Lord Jesus, though we have not seen you, we love you, and though we do not see you now, we believe in you. Fill us with your inexpressible and glorious joy. Amen.

Daily Love Practice

Reflect on the love of Jesus and the hope of salvation, allowing it to fill you with joy that transcends circumstances and brings peace to your soul.Tell someone about how you love Jesus by faith. Describe that love, for yourself and to witness to them your faith.

Day 17

Abide in Christ's Love

As the Father has loved me, so I have loved you;
abide in my love.

John 15:9

Prayer

Ever closer, ever stronger, ever greater, ever pure, let me abide in your love Lord. My heart is your home. My hope is your love. My will is God's will. Amen.

Daily Love Practice

Today, consider how you abide in Jesus' love and act on that abiding by: Reading scripture, attending Church, confession, partaking of Holy Communion, fellowshipping with believers, praising and worshipping, writing a testimony, acting in ways Jesus did for others, serving with compassion or parenting with kindness, generosity and self-control. A glorious day of abiding in Jesus' love even as God the Father has loved him.

Day 18

Christ Died For Us

But God proves his love for us in that while we still were sinners Christ died for us.

Romans 5:8

Prayer

O Lord, thank you for loving me in all my errors, in all my wrong doings, my corruptions, doubt, dishonesty; in all the ways I stumble to perfection. Thank you for loving me in and through my separation from you that I participated in willingly and unwillingly, knowingly and unknowingly. Amen.

Daily Love Practice

God loved us first. He became human and died on the cross so that we could be free and have eternal life. What behaviours do you have that separate you from God that are the definition of sin. Can you hand over a fear, a doubt, a behaviour separating you from his love for you this day?

Day 19

Love the Father

I do as the Father has commanded me, so that the world may know that I love the Father.

John 14:31

Prayer

Into your hands God I commend my spirit. I give it to you with all the love of my heart, for I love you Lord, and I so want to give myself to you with the fullest measure of trust, for you are my God. Amen.

Daily Love Practice

Jesus always points to God the Father as his authority, why? Consider this today. Jesus wants you to have a relationship with God the Trinity, to know God the Father, to obey the commandments, and to have direct experience of God; God's will and grace. Ask the Uncreate God in you, God the Father, to have more God as you commit to doing God's will.

Day 20

He Will Renew You

The Lord your God is in your midst,
a warrior who gives victory;
he will rejoice over you with gladness;
he will renew you by his love;
he will exult over you with loud singing.

Zephaniah 3:17

Prayer

O Lord, hear me as I praise you. I, who have been plucked from worldly affairs, raised up victorious by your might and your mercy. Hear me now as I bow to your love and your will and with heart rejoicing, sing Hallelujah!

Daily Love Practice

Consider the many times God has lifted you up out of situations of the world's making. Notice how God rejoices over you regardless of your circumstances. Feel the love God has for you - all of you, at all times, in all situations. How does knowing and feeling that love impact your relationship with God and your self reflection? Tell a friend.

Day 21

Multiply You

He will love you, bless you, and multiply you.

Deuteronomy 7:13

Prayer

Lord, I give thanks for your provision in all circumstance, the way you love me, bless me and multiply all areas of my life that enrich my life in you. Thank you Lord. Amen.

Daily Love Practice

How have you brought God's love, blessing and provision into your life? Are you giving God opportunities to lift you up in your workplace, family life, relationships? Are you tithing into a ministry that spiritually feeds you? Consider ways you can make yourself more available to God's love, blessings and increase in all areas of your life.

Day 22

Comfort You

Let your steadfast love become my comfort according to your promise to your servant.

Psalm 119:76

Prayer

Lord Jesus, comfort us with your unfailing love, fulfilling the promises you have made to us. May the assurance of your love bring us lasting joy. Amen.

Daily Love Practice

Meditate on God's promises, allowing His unfailing love to bring comfort and joy to your heart throughout the day. 'Steadfast love'. How does this comfort you? What does a promise mean for you—a promise from God? And the word servant—how are you God's servant? Feel all of this within and memorise the verse for times of need.

Day 23

He is Your Strength

I love you, O Lord, my strength.

Psalm 18:1

Prayer

Jesus, my hope and my Saviour, every day your strength raises me up. You are the one I turn to in distress, the one who hears me when I call. You Lord are my refuge, my stronghold and my salvation. You are the rock upon which I stand. I love you Lord with all my heart. Amen.

Daily Love Practice

Read all of Psalm 18 and reflect on the practical ways God strengthens you, and what you offer others through God's strength.

Day 24

With Loyalty

Know, therefore, that the Lord your God is God,
the faithful God who maintains covenant loyalty with
those who love him and keep his commandments.

Deuteronomy 7:9

Prayer

God, my God, search me now for every desire, every deed, every word spoken, see if I am loyal, if I am faithful. Where you find righteousness, let us rejoice O Lord for your grace. Where you find wanting Lord, make me righteousness and true to your covenant. Amen.

Daily Love Practice

Where are you loyal in your life? To what and to whom? Search among your loyalties—Is God present? What are you faithful to that God could come into more?How can you encourage others to keep God's will, to know God's love and the covenant he has with believers? Reflect on this today.

Day 25

With Steadfast Love

The Lord, the Lord, a God merciful and gracious, slow to anger, and abounding in steadfast love and faithfulness.

Exodus 34:6

Prayer

Lord God thank you for your mercy. Lord have mercy on me. Thank you for your patience with me, your mercy, your grace. Thank you for turning all things to righteousness. Amen.

Daily Love Practice

Think of a time when you acted in a way that was not right with God. Maybe you hurt someone, lied, denied God, lost faith, cheated, committed a crime. Now think of where you are today in life. Notice the gap between then and now. Take a moment to ask God to fill that time and that gap with mercy and love. Bathe in that acceptance, that grace for God's everlasting faithfulness to you.

Day 26

He Will Preserve Your Spirit

You have granted me life and steadfast love,
and your care has preserved my spirit.

John 15:10

Prayer

Come Lord, hold my hand. Touch me Lord that I may know and feel your loving embrace. Let us walk together, friends eternal for you are steadfast in your love and I am made whole in my spirit. Amen.

Daily Love Practice

The Lord your God has granted you life. Your life is a gift. What comes to mind when you think of your life as a gift from God? How great the joy is to know that your spirit is preserved for all time safe against death. Think on this for a moment—and with the freedom of certainty allow yourself to take the thought of your life heaven. Glory, glory.

Day 27

For An Eternal Life

Keep yourselves in the love of God; look forward to the mercy of our Lord Jesus Christ that leads to eternal life.

Jude 1:21

Prayer

O God, my Saviour, how great you are. A God of love. A God of mercy. A God who through your love and mercy have granted me eternal life. Thank you Jesus. Amen.

Daily Love Practice

Today, spend the whole day reflecting on your eternal life and salvation. The everyday joy of abiding in Christ's love. The everyday humility that purifies your heart. The everyday grace that pours down upon you. The everyday provision that is God's great gift to you. Marvel and celebrate this today. And let it lead you to do or plan to do something new in God.

Day 28

Love and Good Deeds

And let us consider how to provoke one another to love
and good deeds...

Hebrews 10:24

Prayer

Lord, send me. Let me go about your works in the world, into the places that have need of your Word. Let me be your voice to share the gospel truth, to witness to friends, family, community and strangers your love. By my life and faith, through your grace Lord, let me inspire others to love and good deeds. This I ask in your holy name, Lord Jesus, Amen.

Daily Love Practice

Bring God and praise together to uplift today.The love of God bestowed upon another invites them into Jesus' joy. There, a meeting place of divine energies creates a new work in a person.Be the one to inspire this opportunity for God and others today.

Day 29

Loyalty and Faithfulness

Do not let loyalty and faithfulness forsake you;
bind them around your neck;
write them on the tablet of your heart.

Proverbs 3:3

Prayer

Heavenly Father, imbue my heart with Your steadfast love and faithfulness. Help me to internalise Your love and truth so every action, every decision, every gesture witnesses to those I love and those I am yet to know the very grace and love you bestow upon me, and that is available to them. Amen.

Daily Love Practice

Demonstrate love and faithfulness in a tangible way to someone today. Think about all the ways you are faithful in life, or where you might need God's help with loyalty. Ask for more faithfulness, more loyalty. Ask for new ways to show your faithfulness and loyalty to God, and in your everyday life.

Day 30

Lord Have Mercy

May mercy, peace, and love be yours in abundance.

Jude 1:2

Prayer

Lord Jesus Christ, Son of God, have mercy upon me.
Lord Jesus Christ, Son of God, have mercy upon me.
Lord Jesus Christ, Son of God, have mercy upon me.

Daily Love Practice

Our month ends with the Jesus Prayer. Repeat it gently throughout the day. Notice how your heart opens to Christ, and how Jesus is right there with you. This is a dynamic prayer that unites you with the Spirit of God living inside you. Lord Jesus Christ, Son of God, have mercy upon me. If you only do one prayer a day, this is the one. All else flows from it as you and the Uncreate energies of God become one.

The Fruit of Love

Glory, glory how the illumination of light that is the light of the Trinity shines through each and every prayer. And you, dear one, have dwelt in the room where the Holy of Holies is revealed through your commitment to prayer and the Word of God.

Prayer towards holiness and divine love has pervaded your being this month, deepening your witness of Christ and your faith abiding. The intellect, tamed by the holy light, has proven itself amiable to the grace of God in open acquiescence to union with the indwelling Spirit. The Lord has permitted you to see the purity of your heart as you ventured into emptying yourself of everyday thinking, doing and ways of behaviour, to take up the love that begets godliness.

Every day, we experience the push and pull of emotion. From joy to sadness, hope to disappointment, radiance to despair and back again. A month of living scripture in the energies of the Trinity stabilises that rollercoaster. You'll have noticed this grace. God's steadfast love holds you steady and becomes a focal point for your future.

The wonder of sharing your heart with Jesus in this manner is the presence of heaven that you are privy to as you begin to live God's eternal life for you on earth. You start to live the grace of eternity, your heavenly citizenship right here, right now. And everyone around you benefits. You will have felt some semblance of that beauty, and how the kingdom of God becomes a very real, tangible reality. And you participate in this reality in and through heavenly provision, glorifying God through your life's example. It's a beautiful thing. The most precious of privileges.

Whether you are the disciple who has walked beside Jesus from the time that he first called you, or the prodigal son or daughter who through such grief of separation, has returned home to God's embrace of inexpressible compassion, having abided in God's love this month, you will be filled with a desire to remain in that embrace.

You, who have reflected on God's love in your life, on your salvation, on righteousness, on mercy, on God's providence, on forgiveness, on loving others and keeping true, on defending the gospel and so much more, you have opened the door to Christ anew. And the lover of humankind has met you, hand in hand, and taken you directly to God Almighty that you may know the divine will, obey it and be glorified by it, even as you glorify the Holy Trinity in doing so. What a gift!

In the end, we have learnt a great simplicity—God's love creates our life if we let it. And because God loved us first and loves us still, what God creates for us is always and will always be good and right for us. Let us rise in this wisdom as we pray together the Jesus Prayer—*Lord Jesus Christ, Son of God, have mercy on me.*

As this daily meditation on Love ends, we look to Book 2 and the invitation to partake of the fruit of the Spirit that is Joy. Thank you for being part of this journey in divine Love. Let us continue in faith to pray for God's great mercy and favour.

May God Bless You And Keep You

Appendix A

1. Love God with all your heart, soul, and mind (Matthew 22:37-38). First commandment.
2. Love your neighbour as yourself (Matthew 22:39-40). This is the second most important commandment after loving God.
3. Follow Me (Matthew 4:19). Jesus called His disciples to follow His ways.
4. Let your light shine before others (Matthew 5:16). Encouraging good works to glorify God.
5. Forgive others (Matthew 6:14-15; Mark 11:25). Forgiveness is a central theme in Jesus' teachings.
6. Do not judge others (Matthew 7:1-2). Encouraging a spirit of humility and understanding.

7. Treat others the same way you want them to treat you (Luke 6:31). Often referred to as the Golden Rule.
8. Go and make disciples of all nations (Matthew 28:19-20). Known as the Great Commission, it's a call to evangelise and baptise.
9. Pray then in this way (Matthew 6:9-13). Jesus provides the Lord's Prayer as a model for prayer.
10. Be merciful (Luke 6:36). Jesus emphasises mercy as a core aspect of God's character that His followers should imitate.
11. Do not worry about your life (Matthew 6:25). Encouragement to trust in God's provision.
12. Sell your possessions and give to the poor (Luke 12:33). A call to generosity and detachment from material wealth.

13. Take up your cross and follow Me (Matthew 16:24). A call to discipleship through self-denial and bearing one's burdens.

14. Do not let your hearts be troubled (John 14:1). Encouragement to trust in God and Jesus.

15. Abide in Me, and I in you (John 15:4). The importance of remaining in a close relationship with Jesus.

16. Love one another as I have loved you (John 13:34-35). A new commandment highlighting the depth of love Jesus has for His followers and the love they should have for one another.

17. Repent, for the Kingdom of Heaven is at hand (Matthew 4:17). A call to repentance and spiritual renewal.

18. Seek first His Kingdom and His righteousness (Matthew 6:33). Prioritising God's will and righteousness in one's life.

19. Be reconciled to your brother before offering your gift at the altar (Matthew 5:24). The importance of reconciliation and forgiveness.

20. Do not swear at all (Matthew 5:34-37). Encouraging honesty without the need for oaths.

21. Do not resist an evil person; if someone strikes you on the right cheek, turn to him the other also (Matthew 5:39). Advocating non-violence and forbearance.

22. Give to the one who asks you, and do not turn away from the one who wants to borrow from you (Matthew 5:42). Encouraging generosity and openness to helping others.

23. Love your enemies and pray for those who persecute you (Matthew 5:44). A radical call to love beyond one's community and include enemies.

24. Be perfect, as your heavenly Father is perfect (Matthew 5:48). A call to holiness and moral completeness.

25. Do not store up for yourselves treasures on earth (Matthew 6:19). A teaching against materialism and greed.

26. Do not practice your righteousness in front of others to be seen by them (Matthew 6:1). Encouraging genuine piety rather than performing for human approval.

27. When you pray, go into your room, close the door and pray to your Father, who is unseen (Matthew 6:6).

Instruction on private prayer as a sincere communication with God.

28. Do not be like the hypocrites, for they love to pray standing in the synagogues and on the street corners to be seen by others (Matthew 6:5). Warning against religious hypocrisy.

29. If anyone forces you to go one mile, go with them two miles (Matthew 5:41). Encouraging going above and beyond what is asked.

30. Do not judge, or you too will be judged (Matthew 7:1). A caution against passing judgment on others.

31. Ask, and it will be given to you; seek, and you will find; knock, and the door will be opened to you (Matthew 7:7). Encouragement to persist in prayer and faith.

32. Enter through the narrow gate. For wide is the gate and broad is the road that leads to destruction, and

many enter through it (Matthew 7:13). A call to choose the path of righteousness.

33. Beware of false prophets, who come to you in sheep's clothing but inwardly are ravenous wolves (Matthew 7:15). A warning to be discerning of others' true intentions.

34. Take heed that you do not do your charitable deeds before men, to be seen by them (Matthew 6:1). Encouraging altruism without the need for public recognition.

35. Render to Caesar the things that are Caesar's, and to God the things that are God's (Matthew 22:21). Teaching on the distinction between civic duty and allegiance to God.

36. Whoever wants to become great among you must be your servant (Matthew 20:26). Inverting societal norms of greatness and leadership to service.

37. Do not let your left hand know what your right hand is doing (Matthew 6:3). Encouraging discreet acts of charity.

38. If your eye causes you to stumble, pluck it out and throw it away (Matthew 18:9). A hyperbolic teaching on avoiding sin.

39. Do not give dogs what is sacred; do not throw your pearls to pigs (Matthew 7:6). Instruction on discerning how to share spiritual truths.

40. Whoever does not receive the Kingdom of God like a child will not enter it (Mark 10:15). Encouraging humility and receptiveness as key to entering the Kingdom of God.

41. Do not work for food that spoils, but for food that endures to eternal life (John 6:27). A call to prioritise spiritual sustenance over physical needs.

42. Remain in my love (John 15:9). An invitation to live within the love Christ offers, maintaining a close relationship with Him.

Printed in Great Britain
by Amazon

50431737R00057